CORPORATE RESPONSE TO
ACCELERATED TAX DEPRECIATION:
BONUS DEPRECIATION FOR TAX YEARS 2002-2004

by

Matthew Knittel
Office of Tax Analysis, US Department of Treasury

OTA Working Paper 98   May 2007

OTA Papers is an occasional series of reports on the research, models and datasets developed to inform and improve Treasury's tax policy analysis. The papers are works in progress and subject to revision. Views and opinions expressed are those of the authors and do not necessarily represent official Treasury positions or policy. *OTA Papers* are distributed in order to document OTA analytic methods and data and invite discussion and suggestions for revision and improvement. Comments are welcome and should be directed to the authors.

Office of Tax Analysis
US Department of the Treasury
1500 Pennsylvania Avenue NW
Washington, DC 20220

The author is grateful to Bob Carroll, Don Kiefer, James Mackie, John McClelland, Joel Platt and Laura Power for their helpful comments.

ABSTRACT

This paper examines how corporations responded to temporary accelerated tax depreciation made available by the Jobs Creation and Worker Assistance Act of 2002 and the Jobs and Growth Tax Relief and Reconciliation Act of 2003. Data for tax years 2002 through 2004 reveal that 55 to 63 percent of corporate investment claimed accelerated tax depreciation. Utilization rates were slightly lower for C corporations (54 to 61 percent) than S corporations (65 to 70 percent). The lower C corporation utilization rate may be attributable to net operating losses and tax credits carried forward by C corporations as well as new tax credits. Utilization rates were generally higher for industries where investment is dominated by a relatively small number of firms (e.g., utilities and telecommunications) with longer-lived investment.

I.   INTRODUCTION

On March 9, 2002, President Bush signed the Jobs Creation and Worker Assistance Act of 2002 into law.[1] The Jobs Creation Act provided an additional first-year depreciation allowance equal to 30 percent of the expenditure for eligible investment acquired between September 11, 2001 and September 11, 2004. This provision has been referred to as "bonus" depreciation because it allowed taxpayers to claim a temporary deduction over and above amounts they would ordinarily claim. On May 28, 2003, the Jobs and Growth Tax Relief Reconciliation Act of 2003 increased and extended bonus depreciation.[2] The Jobs and Growth Act increased first-year bonus depreciation to 50 percent for eligible investment acquired after May 5, 2003 and extended bonus depreciation to property acquired before January 1, 2005.[3]

Bonus depreciation reduces the effective tax rate on investment because it allows firms to deduct capital expenditures more quickly. Policymakers hoped that lower tax rates would encourage investment and stimulate economic growth. Using tax data to examine how corporations responded to bonus depreciation, we find that corporations claimed bonus depreciation for 55 to 63 percent of eligible investment. This percentage is referred to as the bonus "take-up" rate. While it is not known what specific factors caused take-up rates to be less than 100 percent, three factors seem particularly relevant: (1) the bonus provision was temporary, (2) many capital intensive firms had losses during this period or carried losses forward from prior tax years (which generally limits the benefit of bonus depreciation), and (3) many states chose not to conform their state tax systems to the federal change.

This paper provides a general retrospective on bonus depreciation. It presents bonus take-up rates across organizational form (C versus S corporation), tax year, tax class of investment and industry. This paper does not address whether bonus depreciation increased investment above levels that would have occurred in its absence. Rather, this paper focuses on the overall utilization of bonus depreciation and the

---

[1] Public Law 107-147.
[2] Public Law 108-27.
[3] For both 30 and 50 percent bonus depreciation, acquired property must be placed in service prior to January 1, 2005.

characteristics of bonus and non-bonus firms. An examination of non-bonus firms reveals certain attributes which may dampen the appeal of accelerated tax depreciation. A better understanding of these attributes may help to inform future investment stimulus proposals.

This paper proceeds as follows. Section Two describes the mechanics of bonus depreciation and the impact of bonus depreciation on firms' effective tax rates. Section Three presents tabulations of corporate tax data by tax year, corporate form, tax class of investment and industry. Section Four concludes with some general observations on bonus depreciation and possible implications for future investment stimulus proposals.

II.   BONUS DEPRECIATION AND INVESTMENT

Policymakers often use temporary tax provisions such as bonus depreciation to elicit a desired response from certain taxpayers. In order to understand the motivation for these provisions, one must consider the circumstances under which they were enacted. The first quarter of 2002 found the U.S. economy emerging slowly from the recession of the previous year. Although broad measures of the economy suggested that the 2001 recession was mild (real gross domestic product increased by 0.8 percent on an annual basis), the recession's impact on the business sector, and in particular, business investment, was more pronounced. From 2000 to 2001, the National Income and Product Accounts record a 10 percent reduction in corporate profits and a 16 percent reduction in equipment and inventory investment.

In an effort to encourage business investment, Congress enacted bonus depreciation. The motivation for bonus depreciation is summarized by the *FY 2004 Economic Report of the President*:

> The tax cuts provided further stimulus by increasing incentives for business investment. Some of these incentives come in the form of bonus depreciation for business investment.... The bonus depreciation was introduced in the 2002 tax cut (JCWAA), which specified that 30 percent of the price of investments made by September 10, 2004 could be treated as an immediate expense under the corporate profits tax and the remaining 70 percent depreciated over time according to the regular depreciation schedules. Moving depreciation closer to the time of new investment increased the

present value of depreciation allowances and the net after-tax return on investment..... These tax changes lowered firms' cost of capital and likely provided support for investment at a crucial time.[4]

Prior to the presentation of tax data, it is useful to examine the mechanism by which accelerated tax depreciation affects the taxpayer's marginal effective tax rate and investment decision. (For the remainder of this paper, we use the term "firm" in lieu of taxpayer.)

A.   *The Mechanics of Bonus Depreciation*

To illustrate the impact of bonus depreciation, Table 1 lists the "regular" tax law and temporary 30 and 50 percent bonus depreciation schedules for the six classes of eligible investment. A simple example demonstrates how bonus depreciation works. Assume that a firm invests $100 in equipment that has a tax life of five years. If the investment qualifies for the 50 percent bonus allowance, then the firm can write-off or deduct 50 percent of the investment in the first year (i.e., $50). The firm then depreciates the remaining amount using the regular depreciation schedule. In this example, the firm would claim another $10 of regular depreciation ($50 times 20 percent), for a total deduction equal to $60 in the first year. Note that if the firm had not claimed bonus depreciation, the deduction would have been $20. Thus, the bonus deduction does not represent the net additional deduction claimed by the firm in the year the investment is made. The additional deduction attributable to the bonus provision is somewhat less than the bonus deduction itself; $40 in this example.

Firms may claim bonus depreciation only for eligible investment. Eligible investment is investment to which the general rules of the Modified Accelerated Cost Recovery System (MACRS) apply that has a class life of 20 years or less.[5] This broad definition generally includes most equipment investment. To qualify for 30 percent bonus depreciation, eligible investment must have been acquired on or after September 11, 2001 and before September 11, 2004. To qualify for 50 percent bonus

---

[4] *FY 2004 Economic Report of the President*, page 45.

[5] For tax purposes, class life refers to the amount of time over which an asset must be depreciated. Under MACRS, there are 9 class lives: 3, 5, 7, 10, 15, 20 25, 27.5 and 39 year property. In addition, taxpayers may be required to use the alternative depreciation system (ADS) or the accelerated cost recovery system (ACRS) depending on the type of assets and the original date of purchase.

depreciation, eligible investment must have been acquired after May 5, 2003 and before January 1, 2005.[6]

Original use must have commenced with the firm claiming the deduction; used equipment purchases did

not qualify for bonus depreciation.[7]

If a firm claims bonus depreciation, it claims a deduction equal to eligible investment multiplied

by the appropriate 30 or 50 percent factor, regardless of when the property was acquired during the tax

year.[8] A firm may elect out of bonus depreciation for any or all classes of eligible investment made

during the tax year. For example, a firm may claim bonus depreciation for twenty-year property, but not

for five-year property. Once a firm elects to forego bonus depreciation, the election for that tax year

cannot be reversed through an amended return. However, an election in one tax year does not constrain a

firm to the same treatment in future years. For example, if a firm does not claim bonus depreciation for

investment made in tax year 2002, it may still claim bonus depreciation for investment made in tax year

2003.

B.   *Impact of Bonus Depreciation on Effective Tax Rates*

Bonus depreciation reduces the effective tax rate on investment because it increases the net

present value of the depreciation allowance. Table 2 shows the net present value of deductions using

regular MACRS depreciation and the 30 and 50 percent bonus depreciation schedules.[9] Bonus

depreciation can substantially accelerate deductions, especially for longer-lived property. Compared to

regular tax depreciation, bonus depreciation increases the net present value of deductions by 18 percent

---

[6] Property is not eligible for 50 percent bonus if there was a binding written contract for the acquisition prior to May 6, 2003. For property placed-in-service after May 5, 2003, taxpayers may elect to use either 30 or 50 percent bonus depreciation.

[7] Eligible investment also includes water utility property, computer software other than software covered by section 197 and qualified leasehold improvement property. The January 1, 2005 placed-in-service date for 30 and 50 percent bonus depreciation was extended one year to January 1, 2006 for property that (1) is produced by a taxpayer and is subject to Code Section 263A uniform capitalization rules, (2) has a production period greater than two years, or greater than one year and a cost exceeding $1 million and (3) has a MACRS recovery period of at least ten years or is used in the trade or business of transporting persons for hire, such as commercial aircraft. The American Jobs Creation Act of 2004 extended the placed-in-service date to January 1, 2006 for certain noncommercial aircraft.

[8] Unlike regular depreciation, bonus depreciation does not use a half-year or mid-quarter convention. These conventions reduce the full-year deduction based on the timing of the purchase during the tax year.

[9] The calculations in Table 2 assume a nominal discount rate of 6.5 percent equal to the real return (3.5 percent) plus inflation (3.0 percent).

(30 percent bonus) and 31 percent (50 percent bonus) for twenty-year property. Conversely, for three-year property, bonus depreciation adds little to net present values: one and two percent respectively.

Although present value comparisons are straightforward and can be informative, they do not provide a comprehensive measure of the impact that accelerated tax depreciation has on investment incentives.[10] A more complete measure is a firm's marginal effective tax rate which is a derivative of the cost of capital as first developed by Hall and Jorgensen (1967). The cost of capital is the pre-tax rate of return on a barely profitable investment that covers the investment's tax cost while still leaving the investor his or her required after-tax rate of return. The cost of capital represents the pre-tax return on the final or marginal investment; firms should undertake additional investment as long as the (net of depreciation) marginal product of capital exceeds the cost of capital.[11]

Based on the formula originally derived by Hall and Jorgensen, a simplified version of the cost of capital may be expressed as follows:

(1) $p = (r + d)(1 - uz) / (1 - u) - d$

where r is equal to the real discount rate, d is the economic rate of depreciation, u is the statutory corporate income tax rate and z is the present discounted value of allowances for tax depreciation for one dollar of investment. As shown by equation (1), faster write-off of investment reduces the cost of capital by increasing the present value of depreciation (z). We note that this simple cost of capital formula: (1) assumes that firms have sufficient tax liability to utilize all deductions, (2) ignores state and local taxes, and (3) assumes that firms do not resell assets.

Table 2 depicts the impact of bonus depreciation on firms' cost of capital for the six classes of eligible investment. Following Brazell and Mackie (2002), the computations assume that investments are held forever and two-fifths of investment is financed by debt, the remainder with equity which is split

---

[10] For example, bonus depreciation does not significantly increase investment incentives for longer-lived assets compared to short-lived assets, as is misleadingly suggested by the computation of present value of deductions.
[11] As noted by Cohen et al. (2002), this condition assumes that the following conditions apply: (1) zero adjustment or installation costs, (2) no time required to build or plan additions to the capital stock and (3) taxpayers expect tax laws to remain unchanged.

between retained earnings and new share issues.[12] (In equation (1), the method of financing affects r and is not explicitly visible.) The computations assume that the required real return to investment is equal to 3.5 percent and inflation equals three percent. The computations also include the effects of taxes at the investor level: we set individual/investor level tax rates at 14.5 percent for capital gains, 16.5 percent for dividends and 22.5 percent for interest income.[13] [14]

Using these assumptions, the marginal effective tax rate is then equal to the difference between the cost of capital (p) and the required return on investment (s) divided by the cost of capital or $(p - s) / p$. The marginal effective tax rate is the tax rate that, if levied on economic income, would be equivalent in its incentive effects to the various features of the tax code modeled in the cost of capital formula, such as depreciation, statutory tax rates at the entity and investor levels and indexing provisions (Brazell and Mackie, 2002).[15] If the tax system measured and taxed economic income, then the marginal effective tax rate on investment would equal the statutory tax rate.[16] [17]

---

[12] The computations assume that retained earnings comprise 93 percent of equity's share and new issues comprise 7 percent.

[13] These rates are "average marginal" tax rates from the Treasury individual income tax simulation model for tax law effective for tax year 2004. For example, the dividend tax rate of 16.5 percent (mix of qualified and non-qualified) implies that tax receipts would increase by $16.5 billion if dividends were increased by $100 billion and pro-rated across all individuals that held dividends in the sample. Qualified dividends received after December 31, 2002 are taxed at the same rate as an individual's long-term capital gains. For long-term capital gains reported for tax year 2004, the tax rate is 5 percent for individuals in the 10 or 15 percent income tax brackets and 15 percent otherwise. The long-term gains rate falls to zero for individuals in the 10 and 15 percent income tax brackets for tax years 2009-2011. For tax year 2012, the long-term gains rate reverts to pre-2003 law: 10 percent (10 or 15 percent income tax bracket) or 20 percent (all others). We further reduce the capital gains tax rate to account for deferral and tax-free step-up at death. Rates are not adjusted to account for any tax-exempt ownership of assets.

[14] These computations assume implicitly that bonus depreciation is permanent. For a discussion of the effects of temporary partial expensing on investment incentives, see Cohen and et al. (2002). The authors find that temporary stimulus provides greater investment incentives than permanent stimulus.

[15] Economic income is generally defined as consumption plus change in wealth. For corporate profits, economic income implies that assets would be depreciated using economic depreciation and would be marked-to-market each year.

[16] For example, if the investment were equity financed and there were no shareholder level taxes, then the marginal effective tax rate would equal the statutory tax rate on corporate income (u). Accelerated depreciation would reduce the marginal effective tax rate below u. Debt finance typically would reduce the marginal effective tax rate below u because the lender's tax rate typically is below u. By contrast, the double tax on corporate profits (i.e., shareholder taxes on dividends and capital gains) would raise the marginal effective tax rate.

[17] Under certain conditions, it is possible for the marginal effective tax rate on investment to be negative. This result will occur for debt-financed investments where borrowers face higher tax rates than lenders, interest is not indexed for inflation or tax depreciation is very accelerated (e.g., expensing). In those cases, the after-tax return on investment exceeds the pre-tax return.

Marginal effective tax rates are shown in the final columns of Table 2. Compared to regular tax law, 30 percent bonus depreciation reduces the marginal effective tax rate by 12-21 percent; 50 percent bonus depreciation reduces the rate by 21-37 percent. Most eligible investment (approximately 75-78 percent of outlays) is for five and seven-year property where 30 percent bonus depreciation reduces the marginal effective tax rate by 17-18 percent and 50 percent bonus depreciation reduces the rate by 29-32 percent.

C.   Cash Flow Benefit of Bonus Depreciation

Marginal effective tax rates are useful when considering the firm's investment decision, but they do not provide insight regarding bonus depreciation's cash flow benefit to a firm. Table 3 shows the maximum potential benefit to firms who claim bonus depreciation for a $1 million investment. The computed cash flow benefit is simply the net present value of the change in tax liability over the tax life of the investment. For example, bonus depreciation on a $1 million investment in five-year property would reduce tax liability by $140,000 in the year of investment: $600,000 times 35 percent less $200,000 times 35 percent. Bonus depreciation then increases tax liability by $56,000 in the second year, $34,000 in the third year, $20,000 in the fourth and fifth years and $10,000 in the sixth year (a net differential of zero if we ignore present value). The net present value of this change in tax liability over the investment's tax life ($13,700) yields the firm's cash flow benefit from delaying tax payments. Such figures are relevant for firms that are merely deciding whether to claim bonus depreciation, as opposed to firms deciding whether to increase investment in response to the temporary stimulus.

For three-year property, the computed cash flow benefit is quite modest ($6,400). The cash flow benefit more than doubles ($13,700) for five-year property. For twenty-year property, the cash flow benefit is significant ($64,500) because bonus depreciation pulls deductions forward from tax years many years in the future. It should be noted that the cash flow benefit appears much larger for longer-lived property largely due to the asset's longer tax life for a given outlay. If a similar comparison were made between a single $1 million investment in twenty-year property and four $1 million investments in five-year property over a twenty-year period, the cash flow benefit difference would be much smaller.

These simple cash flow computations assume that firms have sufficient taxable income to make full use of all accelerated deductions in the first year of bonus depreciation. However, this assumption does not hold for many firms. For example, loss firms cannot immediately use the accelerated deduction to offset taxable income and must instead carry the loss forward to offset taxable income in a future year.[18] Alternatively, firms with stocks of unused credits or loss carryforwards may receive less benefit from bonus depreciation if the accelerated deduction merely displaces a credit or loss carryforward that would have been claimed in its absence. For carryforward firms and firms that generate new tax credits, it is possible that bonus depreciation has little or no impact on the stream of tax liability reported by the firm.

Table 3 lists the cash flow benefit if the additional bonus depreciation allowances cannot be used to offset taxable income for one or two tax years. This delay may effectively occur if the firm reports a tax loss or if the firm had loss carryforwards or credits that could have been used to offset taxable income. For three-year property, a one-year delay reduces the cash flow benefit by 54 percent; a two-year delay reduces the benefit by 90 percent. For five-year and seven-year property, a one-year delay reduces the cash flow benefit by 20-30 percent; a two-year delay by 50-65 percent. For fifteen and twenty-year property, a one-year delay reduces the cash flow benefit by only 8-10 percent; a two-year delay by 22-26 percent.

Given these computations, a pertinent question is: what was the cash flow benefit for a typical firm claiming bonus depreciation? For tax year 2004, the median level of eligible investment for C corporations claiming bonus depreciation in our dataset was $215,000. If we assume that (1) a firm can immediately use the accelerated deduction to offset taxable income, (2) the deduction does not displace a loss carryforward or credit that would otherwise be claimed, (3) the firm pays tax at 35 percent, and (4) the firm invests in five-year property, then the cash flow benefit from bonus depreciation was

---

[18] However, it is possible that the firm could also carry the loss back to offset tax liability from the prior two tax years. If the firm is able to carry the entire loss back, then the tax benefit of bonus deprecation is not muted.

approximately $3,000 for the median firm. We note that the cash flow benefit will be significantly higher for a small number of firms that report the majority of tax investment.[19]

III. CORPORATE TAX DATA

The data used for this analysis are from the IRS' Statistics of Income (SOI) corporate income tax files for tax years 2002 through 2004. The data file for each tax year is a stratified sample of returns for C and S corporations with tax years ending July of year t through June of year t+1. For example, tax year 2002 includes firms with tax years that end in July 2002 through June 2003.

For the tabulations that appear in this paper, we use a subset of the SOI annual samples. The subset is composed of firms that report at least $100,000 of total depreciation allowances for the tax year. This depreciation floor serves two purposes. First, it screens out many small firms that may neglect to supply relevant detail on their tax return. Second, the floor minimizes the impact from changes to Section 179 expensing thresholds. The Jobs and Growth Tax Relief Reconciliation Act of 2003 increased the Section 179 expensing limit from $24,000 for tax year 2002 to $100,000 for tax year 2003 and $102,000 for tax year 2004. Small firms eligible to use Section 179 expensing would not claim bonus depreciation because the treatment is less generous than full expensing. Although the depreciation floor eliminates most firms that claim Section 179 expensing, the final dataset does retain some of these firms.[20] [21]

Table 4 compares our dataset to the entire corporate population and the SOI corporate sample. For tax year 2004, 5.5 million corporations filed tax returns: 2.0 million C corporations and 3.5 million S corporations. The SOI corporate sample that is weighted to produce population totals includes 128,839 firms: 78,746 C corporations and 50,093 S corporations. For tax year 2004, corporations claimed $168 billion of bonus depreciation deductions. Although our dataset includes only five percent of firms from

---

[19] For tax year 2004, the top fifty C corporations ranked by eligible investment reported approximately one-third of total eligible investment for that entity type; the top one hundred firms reported approximately 46 percent of total eligible investment.

[20] The exclusion of these firms has a very minor effect on overall bonus take-up rates for both C and S corporations.

[21] See Knittel (2005) for a discussion of how small firms utilized Section 179 expensing and bonus depreciation for tax years 2002-2003.

the corporate population (and 55 percent of firms from the SOI sample), it does capture approximately 95 percent of total bonus deductions because it includes all large firms.

A.   *Computation of Eligible Investment*

Firms claim depreciation allowances on Form 4562, Depreciation and Amortization, which accompanies the filing of corporate income tax Form 1120. On Form 4562, firms list the deduction attributable to bonus depreciation, regular MACRS deductions for assets placed in service during prior tax years, and regular MACRS deductions for assets place in service during the tax year just ended. Next to the deduction for new investment, firms report the basis for each class of property: 3, 5, 7, 10, 15, 20 and 25-year property as well as residential and non-residential rental properties (tax life more than 25 years). Because bonus depreciation is claimed first, reported basis amounts are net of any bonus depreciation.

In order to gauge how intensively firms used bonus depreciation, we must compute total investment that is eligible for the additional deduction. Eligible investment includes investment in new equipment that has a tax life between three and twenty years. Most of the data necessary to make this computation are reported by firms on Form 4562. However, there are two notable exceptions. First, firms do not report how much of their current year investment is new (eligible) versus used (not eligible). The Annual Capital Expenditures Survey published by the Census Bureau indicates that approximately five percent of all equipment sales are purchases of used equipment. For the purposes of this analysis, we deflate our computed eligible investment figures by five percent to remove used assets. If this adjustment is overstated (understated), then it will imply that our estimates of bonus take-up rates are also overstated (understated).

Second, although we use a screen to eliminate small firms from the dataset, reporting issues remain for some firms. A small number of firms report total depreciation but do not provide certain investment detail because the tax return will be amended and re-submitted at some later point. If the firm did not report any current year investment (i.e., basis amounts were blank), then we impute investment for these firms. For firms that claimed bonus depreciation, this computation was straightforward: we assume that eligible investment is equal to the grossed-up bonus deduction. For example, if the firm claimed $100 of bonus depreciation but did not report any eligible investment, then we assume that eligible investment was equal to $100 divided by 50 percent or $200 (for 2004). For firms that did not claim bonus depreciation, we impute an amount based on the reported total depreciation deduction for the year. Overall, this investment imputation increased total eligible investment by approximately 10 percent.[22]

B.   *Bonus Depreciation: C Corporations*

Table 5 presents tabulations for C corporations for tax years 2002 – 2004 grouped based on tax year and bonus status (claim or do not claim). For tax year 2002, 61 percent of firms in our dataset claimed bonus depreciation (30 percent bonus effective for the entire tax year). Although the bonus allowance increased to 50 percent by tax year 2004, the share of firms claiming bonus fell slightly (59 percent). The slight reduction in the participation rate was attributable to the increase in the Section 179 expensing thresholds. Firms eligible to expense investments under the higher Section 179 thresholds did so rather than claim bonus depreciation.

For tax years 2002-2004, computed eligible investment declined from $492 billion to $460 billion (-7 percent). For all tax years, bonus firms reported approximately 78 percent of total eligible investment. Bonus depreciation deductions increased from $80 billion for tax year 2002 to $140 billion for tax year 2004 (76 percent). If the bonus depreciation deduction is grossed up by the relevant bonus factor, we derive the amount of investment that used bonus depreciation. For tax year 2002, the bonus factor is equal to 30 percent since that allowance was effective for nearly the entire tax year.[23] For tax year 2003, the relevant bonus factor is less straightforward because some investment qualified for 30 percent bonus depreciation while other investment qualified for 50 percent bonus depreciation. We use a weighted

---

[22] Approximately 75 to 78 percent of eligible investment is investment in five or seven-year property. If a firm only invests in five-year property and investment is flat over a five-year period, then depreciation claimed in the fifth year would equal new investment in that year. If investment increases slightly over the five-year period, then investment would slightly exceed total depreciation claimed in the fifth year. For firms that do not provide investment detail, we assume that investment is equal to 80 percent of claimed depreciation. This ratio is generally consistent with firms that do report investment detail.

[23] The only exception is firms with tax years that end in May or June 2003 who made the investment after May 5, 2003. Those firms could claim 50 percent bonus depreciation for that investment. Because the great majority of investment is reported by firms that have tax years that do not end in May or June, we assume those amounts are very small.

average factor of 43.8 percent for tax year 2003.[24] For tax year 2004, 50 percent bonus depreciation was effective for the entire tax year.

Having computed the amount of investment that used bonus depreciation, we then derive bonus "take-up" rates. The bonus take-up rate is equal to the ratio of investment that used bonus to total eligible investment. Aggregate take-up rates for C corporations are as follows: 54 percent for tax year 2002, 58 percent for tax year 2003 and 61 percent for tax year 2004.

The aggregate take-up rate for all firms is a weighted average rate for bonus and non-bonus firms. Aggregate take-up rates are less than 100 percent because many firms did not claim bonus depreciation and some bonus firms did not fully use the provision. As shown by Table 5, take-up rates for bonus firms ranged from 71 to 77 percent; they are not 100 percent. The partial utilization of bonus depreciation might be attributable to a variety of factors. Firms might claim bonus depreciation only for certain classes of property, such as longer-lived property, where the cash flow benefit is greatest. Alternatively, firms might have subsidiaries that elected to claim bonus depreciation while other subsidiaries did not. Finally, it is possible that these firms had significant investment in used assets that is not eligible for bonus depreciation. For such firms, the five percent deflator we use for used equipment would be too small an adjustment and the firm would appear to underutilize the provision.[25]

The tabulations from the bottom of Table 5 suggest two possible explanations as to why firms did not claim bonus depreciation. First, non-bonus firms were clearly less profitable (on a tax basis) compared to firms that claimed bonus depreciation. Average net income for bonus firms was considerably higher than non-bonus firms. As noted above, the cash flow benefit of bonus depreciation is smaller for loss firms because they cannot immediately use the accelerated deduction. Second, non-bonus

---

[24] For each tax year, corporate taxpayers can be divided into 12 groups based on the month their tax year ends. Each group will have a different number of months that 30 and 50 percent bonus was effective. For example, firms with tax years ending December 2003 had 30 percent bonus for 4 months and 50 percent bonus for 8 months, yielding an average of 43.3 percent. This average is computed for all twelve groups. Those amounts are then weighted by each group's share of eligible investment for the tax year. We note that this computation assumes that investment is evenly distributed throughout the tax year.

[25] It is also possible that firms continued to claim bonus depreciation at 30 percent rather than 50 percent in tax years 2003 and 2004. However, these firms still underutilize the provision.

firms relied relatively more on other means to reduce or eliminate tax liability. For non-bonus firms, net operating loss deductions (NOLDs) and tax credits reduced tax liability by approximately 60 percent. For bonus firms, the comparable figure is 30 percent. Firms with stocks of unused credits or loss carryforwards have less incentive to claim bonus depreciation because the corresponding tax benefit is smaller. Bonus depreciation might simply displace a credit or loss carryforward that must now be claimed in a future tax year.[26]

C.   *Bonus Depreciation: S Corporations*

Table 6 reproduces the tabulations from Table 5 for S corporations. The share of firms claiming bonus depreciation was flat from tax year 2002 to 2004 (71 versus 70 percent). S corporations claiming bonus depreciation reported approximately 80 percent of total eligible investment. Aggregate take-up rates ranged from 65 to 70 percent, slightly higher than C corporations. Bonus firms were generally larger (as measured by average eligible investment) and more profitable (as measured by average net income).

D.   *Bonus Take-Up Rates Across Investment Classes*

Because temporary bonus depreciation has the greatest impact on cash flows for longer-lived property, one would expect that take-up rates increase with the tax life of the investment. Table 7 displays bonus take-up rates across the six eligible classes of investment for C corporations. As noted, five and seven-year property comprise the majority of eligible investment; approximately 75-78 percent for all tax years. Five-year property includes cars, light and heavy general-purpose trucks, qualified technological equipment, semi-conductor manufacturing equipment, computers and peripheral equipment and office machinery. Seven-year property includes office furniture and equipment that is not structural in nature, assets used in commercial and contract carrying of passengers and freight by air, certain livestock and machinery and equipment used in agricultural activities. All remaining eligible investment

---

[26] In addition, some credits or loss carryforwards might expire if unused. Expiration is unlikely for loss carryforwards and general business credits as they expire after 20 years. However, this explanation may be pertinent for foreign tax credits, which expire after five years if unused. The American Jobs Creation Act of 2004 extends the carryforward period to 10 years for foreign tax credits arising in tax years after October 22, 2004.

is composed of three-year property (certain software and rent-to-own property), ten-year property (vessels and barges, certain agricultural structures and trees or vines that bear nuts or fruits), fifteen-year property (telephone and telegraph equipment, gas facilities and certain engines and turbines) and twenty-year property (electric light and power facilities, railroads and farm structures).

Similar to the overall average, take-up rates for each class of eligible investment increased between tax years 2002 and 2004. The data do not suggest a strong relationship between average take-up rates and the tax life of the investment. For all tax years, the average take-up rate for five-year property was slightly above the overall average. Conversely, the average take-up rate for fifteen-year and twenty-year property was below the overall average for two of three years. This result is likely attributable to the commingling of firms with different tax attributes within each investment class (e.g., the combination of profit and loss firms). [27]

E.   *Bonus Take-Up Rates Across Industries*

Compared to tabulations based on the tax life of the investment, average industry take-up rates reveal greater dispersion. Table 8 presents average take-up rates for 19 industries ranked in ascending order by that metric. Industries composed of small firms with low average levels of investment (agriculture, real estate and rental (excludes autos), and construction) tend to have lower take-up rates compared to industries where investment is heavily concentrated in a few large firms (utilities, information-telecommunications and transportation equipment manufacturing). This result is intuitive because firms must incur fixed costs to claim bonus depreciation, such as learning how the provision works and alterations to firm-specific tax software programs. [28] If the firm is a multi-state firm, then any fixed costs might be higher because many states decoupled from bonus depreciation and disallowed it for

---

[27] To derive the splits used in Table 7, it is necessary to attribute the bonus deduction to the tax class from which it arose. Firms do not report explicitly the investment composition of the bonus deduction reported on the tax return; only the total bonus deduction is reported. For the purposes of the computations in Table 7, we assume that bonus depreciation is apportioned in a manner similar to the residual basis amounts that firms do report on Form 4562 for each property class. For example, if 20 percent of the total residual basis (post-bonus) was attributable to 7-year property, we assume the same split for bonus depreciation.

[28] In addition, firm size could serve as a proxy for sophistication. Large firms have tax departments that are well-informed regarding all new tax provisions. By contrast, small firms may not have personnel dedicated solely to tax issues.

state income tax purposes. For many multi-state firms, it may have been necessary to compute tax depreciation both with and without the bonus allowance on a state-by-state basis. Data from the Commerce Clearing House show that only 14 out of 46 states with a corporate income tax fully conformed to the federal provision. Of the non-conforming states, 21 states completely disallowed bonus depreciation and 11 states required taxpayers to add back some portion of the bonus deduction.

IV.   OBSERVATIONS AND CONCLUSIONS

This paper examines the corporate response to bonus depreciation for tax years 2002-2004. We find that corporate take-up rates ranged from 54 to 61 percent for C corporations and 65 to 70 percent for S corporations. Take-up rates rose only slightly when the bonus factor increased from 30 to 50 percent. An interesting result is that we did not observe a stronger relationship between take-up rates and average tax life of investment. Even for utilities where eligible investment has an average tax life of 16.6 years, the bonus take-up rate for tax year 2004 was only 67 percent.[29]

We discuss several plausible explanations for why C corporations opted to forgo bonus depreciation. For some firms, bonus depreciation may have afforded little, if any, benefit. Specifically, loss firms, firms with loss or credit carryforwards and firms that generate new credits may realize little cash flow benefit. A closer inspection of large non-bonus firms (firms with eligible investment exceeding $1 billion) for tax year 2004 reveals that nearly all firms reported a tax loss or used a loss carryforward or foreign tax credit to eliminate tax liability. Due to their complexity and relatively short life (five years), firms may have been reluctant to displace a foreign tax credit with temporary bonus depreciation. We also noted that most states disallowed bonus depreciation for state income tax purposes. Although we cannot quantify the impact of those actions, they likely reduced bonus take-up rates.

Despite these explanations, there remain inexplicable cases of non-bonus firms that have significant tax liabilities. While the reasons for this outcome are not immediately clear, it is consistent

---

[29] For utilities, one explanation for the lower-than-expected bonus take-up rate could be the interaction with rate-of-return regulation. Bonus depreciation would alter expected or projected tax payments and possibly affect the formula for determining a utility's revenue requirement.

with the corporate response to the implementation of the Asset Depreciation Range (ADR) system in 1971. The Revenue Act of 1971 provided a range of asset lives for various classes of assets placed in service after December 1970. The Revenue Act of 1971 allowed firms to use shorter asset lives than provided for under prior law. Although more generous depreciation allowances were made available, Vasquez (1974) found that many firms elected not to use the ADR system and instead used less generous schedules that decreased the present value of deductions. Even among large firms, Vasquez found that only 63 percent of firms elected to use the ADR system. Similar to our results, Vasquez found higher utilization rates for industries dominated by large firms with longer-lived property.

What lessons can be inferred from these data? This analysis suggests that the bonus factor was not high enough to induce firms with two-fifths of corporate investment to improve their cash flow by deferring tax liability to a future year. The bonus factor may not have been high enough to offset loss status, credits and loss carryforwards that may dampen the appeal of temporary accelerated depreciation. This fact is especially relevant if the policy is used when the economy is emerging from recession, as many large firms will have generated stocks of loss and credit carryforwards.

In addition to the bonus factor, another key parameter of temporary investment stimulus is the length of the time that accelerated depreciation is made available. Tax data are less helpful in assessing this parameter. Bonus depreciation spanned three and one-quarter years from September 11, 2001 to December 31, 2004.[30] It is not clear whether bonus depreciation would have been more or less effective if allowed for a shorter time interval. Despite the uncertainty, policymakers should be aware that providing firms with too much time to react to temporary investment stimulus could dilute its impact. In order to realize the full immediate benefit of temporary investment stimulus, investment that will be "pulled forward" from future time periods when stimulus is not available should occur sooner rather than later. If the temporary provision is available over a number of years, then this pull forward effect could be delayed.

---

[30] However, bonus depreciation was applied retroactively to investment made between September 2001 and March 2002.

REFERENCES

Brazell, David W., and Mackie, James B. "Depreciation Lives and Methods: Current Issues in the U.S. Capital Cost Recovery System." *National Tax Journal* 53 No. 3 (June 1991): 531-561.

Cohen, Darrel S., Hansen, Dorthe-Pernille and Hassett, Kevin A. "The Effects of Temporary Partial Expensing on Investment Incentives in the United States." *National Tax Journal* 55 No. 3 (September, 2002): 457 – 466.

Cohen, Darrel and Cummins, Jason. "A Retrospective Evaluation of the Effects of Temporary Partial Expensing." Finance and Economics Discussion Series, Federal Reserve Board, Washington D.C., No. 2006-19.

Fullerton, Don. "The Indexation of Interest, Depreciation, and Capital Gains: A Model of Investment Incentives." NBER Working Paper No. 1655. June 1985.

Gravelle, Jane E. "Whither Tax Depreciation." *National Tax Journal* 54 No. 3 (September, 2002): 513 – 526.

Hall, Robert E., and Dale W. Jorgensen. "Tax Policy and Investment Behavior." *American Economic Review* 57 No. 3 (June, 1967): 391-414.

Hulten, Charles R., and Frank C. Wykoff. "The Measurement of Economic Depreciation." In *Depreciation, Inflation and the Taxation of Income from Capital*, edited by Charles R. Hulten. Washington D.C.: The Urban Institute Press, 1981.

Knittel, Matthew. "Small Business Utilization of Accelerated Tax Depreciation: Section 179 Expensing and Bonus Depreciation." *Proceedings of the National Tax Journal, Ninety-Eighth Annual Conference,* Fall 2005, p. 273 – 286.

Vasquez, Thomas. "The Effects of the Asset Depreciation Range System on Depreciation Practices." OTA Working Paper 1, May 1974. Office of Tax Analysis, US Department of Treasury.

Table 1: Regular MACRS and Bonus Depreciation Schedules

	2002	2003	2004	2005	2006	2007	2008	2009	2010	2011	2012	2013	2014	2015	2016	2017
Regular MACRS Depreciation Schedule (half-year convention)																
3 yr property	33.3	44.5	14.8	7.4												
5 yr property	20.0	32.0	19.2	11.5	11.5	5.8										
7 yr property	14.3	24.5	17.5	12.5	8.9	8.9	8.9	4.5								
10 yr property	10.0	18.0	14.4	11.5	9.2	7.4	6.6	6.6	6.6	6.6	3.3					
15 yr property	5.0	9.5	8.6	7.7	6.9	6.2	5.9	5.9	5.9	5.9	5.9	5.9	5.9	5.9	5.9	3.0
20 yr property	3.8	7.2	6.7	6.2	5.7	5.3	4.9	4.5	4.5	4.5	4.5	4.5	4.5	4.5	4.5	4.5
Modified Schedule with 30 Percent Bonus Depreciation																
3 yr property	53.3	31.1	10.4	5.2												
5 yr property	44.0	22.4	13.4	8.1	8.1	4.0										
7 yr property	40.0	17.1	12.2	8.7	6.3	6.2	6.3	3.1								
10 yr property	37.0	12.6	10.1	8.1	6.5	5.2	4.6	4.6	4.6	4.6	2.3					
15 yr property	33.5	6.7	6.0	5.4	4.9	4.4	4.1	4.1	4.1	4.1	4.1	4.1	4.1	4.1	4.1	2.1
20 yr property	32.6	5.1	4.7	4.3	4.0	3.7	3.4	3.2	3.1	3.1	3.1	3.1	3.1	3.1	3.1	3.1
Modified Schedule with 50 Percent Bonus Depreciation																
3 yr property	66.7	22.2	7.4	3.7												
5 yr property	60.0	16.0	9.6	5.8	5.8	2.9										
7 yr property	57.1	12.2	8.7	6.2	4.5	4.5	4.5	2.2								
10 yr property	55.0	9.0	7.2	5.8	4.6	3.7	3.3	3.3	3.3	3.3	1.6					
15 yr property	52.5	4.8	4.3	3.9	3.5	3.1	3.0	3.0	3.0	3.0	3.0	3.0	3.0	3.0	3.0	1.5
20 yr property	51.9	3.6	3.3	3.1	2.9	2.6	2.4	2.3	2.2	2.2	2.2	2.2	2.2	2.2	2.2	2.2

Note: Depreciation for twenty-year property continues for an additional five years.

Table 2: Cost of Capital and Marginal Effective Tax Rates

Tax Life	Present Value of Deduction (1)			Cost of Capital			Marginal Effective Tax Rate		
	MACRS	30% Bonus	50% Bonus	MACRS	30% Bonus	50% Bonus	MACRS	30% Bonus	50% Bonus
3 year	93.2	94.3	95.0	4.9%	4.7%	4.5%	28.7%	25.3%	22.8%
5 year	89.0	91.4	92.9	4.8%	4.5%	4.3%	26.8%	22.3%	19.1%
7 year	85.0	88.6	90.9	4.8%	4.5%	4.3%	27.5%	22.4%	18.7%
10 year	79.5	84.7	88.2	4.8%	4.5%	4.2%	26.7%	21.3%	17.3%
15 year	67.4	76.3	82.1	4.8%	4.4%	4.2%	26.3%	20.7%	16.4%
20 year	60.0	71.1	78.4	5.0%	4.6%	4.3%	29.5%	23.3%	18.4%

(1) Assumes discount rate of 6.5 percent.

Table 3: Cash Flow Benefit from Bonus Depreciation
$1 million eligible investment, 50 percent bonus depreciation

Tax Class	Immediate Use (1)	Delay One Year	Delay Two Years
3-year property	6,400	2,900	700
5-year property	13,700	9,500	4,700
7-year property	20,700	16,200	10,100
10-year property	30,400	25,700	18,500
15-year property	51,500	46,600	38,000
20-year property	64,500	59,500	50,600

(1) Assumes discount rate of 6.5 percent.

Table 4: Corporate Tax Data
tax years, billions of dollars

	2002			2003			2004		
	All	C Corps	S Corps	All	C Corps	S Corps	All	C Corps	S Corps
All Firms									
Number Firms	5,254,451	2,100,074	3,154,377	5,389,199	2,047,593	3,341,606	5,545,947	2,027,613	3,518,334
Number Sample Firms (unweighted)	127,439	80,007	47,432	123,967	78,407	45,560	128,839	78,746	50,093
Bonus Depreciation Deductions	96	82	14	134	114	20	168	143	25
Corporate Tax After Credits	153	153	0	177	177	0	220	219	0
Dataset: Firms with Depreciation > $100,000									
Number Firms	254,118	129,680	124,438	262,355	137,295	125,060	257,336	133,158	124,178
Number Sample Firms (unweighted)	69,008	44,750	24,258	67,848	44,031	23,817	69,091	43,439	25,652
Bonus Depreciation Deductions	90	80	10	128	112	16	162	140	23
Corporate Tax After Credits	142	141	0	166	165	0	211	210	0
Dataset Share									
Number Firms	5%	6%	4%	5%	7%	4%	5%	7%	4%
Number Sample Firms (unweighted)	54%	56%	51%	55%	56%	52%	54%	55%	51%
Bonus Depreciation Deductions	94%	98%	74%	96%	98%	80%	96%	98%	89%
Corporate Tax After Credits	92%	92%	90%	94%	94%	83%	96%	96%	80%

Table 5: Tax Data for C Corporations
tax years, billions of dollars

	All Firms			Firms Claiming Bonus			Firms Not Claiming Bonus		
	2002	2003	2004	2002	2003	2004	2002	2003	2004
Number Firms	129,680	137,295	133,158	79,638	80,996	77,957	50,042	56,299	55,201
Eligible Investment (1)	492	449	460	373	353	367	119	96	93
Bonus Depreciation	80	112	140	80	112	140	0	0	0
Bonus Factor	30%	44%	50%	30%	44%	50%	30%	44%	50%
Investment Using Bonus	265	257	280	265	257	280	0	0	0
Bonus Take-Up Rate (2)	54%	58%	61%	71%	73%	77%	0%	0%	0%
Net Income	265	454	705	326	462	630	-60	-9	75
Positive Net Income	617	719	911	476	567	715	141	152	197
Negative Net Income	-352	-266	-206	-150	-105	-84	-201	-161	-122
Tax After Credits	141	165	210	119	143	180	22	22	31
Average Levels (millions)									
Eligible Investment (1)	3.8	3.3	3.5	4.7	4.4	4.7	2.4	1.7	1.7
Net Income	2.0	3.3	5.3	4.1	5.7	8.1	-1.2	-0.2	1.4
Tax After Credits	1.1	1.2	1.6	1.5	1.8	2.3	0.4	0.4	0.6

(1) Assumes used equipment comprises 5 percent of total equipment investment.
(2) When computing bonus take-up rates, we exclude eligible investment that used Section 179 expensing because that deduction is claimed prior to bonus depreciation. Section 179 deductions for firms included in our dataset were as follows: $0.6 billion (2002), $3.3 billion (2003), and $4.2 billion (2004).

Table 6: Tax Data for S Corporations
tax years, billions of dollars

	All Firms			Firms Claiming Bonus			Firms Not Claiming Bonus		
	2002	2003	2004	2002	2003	2004	2002	2003	2004
Number Firms	124,438	125,060	124,178	88,265	82,622	86,785	36,173	42,438	37,393
Eligible Investment (1)	53	58	67	40	46	55	13	12	12
Bonus Depreciation	10	16	23	10	16	23	0	0	0
Bonus Factor	30%	44%	50%	30%	44%	50%	30%	44%	50%
Investment Using Bonus	34	36	45	34	36	45	0	0	0
Bonus Take-Up Rate (2)	65%	65%	70%	86%	84%	87%	0%	0%	0%
Net Income	59	64	83	55	57	72	4	7	11
Positive Net Income	82	87	106	69	71	88	13	16	18
Negative Net Income	-23	-23	-23	-14	-15	-15	-9	-8	-7
Average Levels (millions)									
Eligible Investment (1)	0.4	0.5	0.5	0.5	0.6	0.6	0.4	0.3	0.3
Net Income	0.5	0.5	0.7	0.6	0.7	0.8	0.1	0.2	0.3

(1) Assumes used equipment comprises 5 percent of total equipment investment.
(2) When computing bonus take-up rates, we exclude eligible investment that used Section 179 expensing because that deduction is claimed prior to bonus depreciation. Section 179 deductions for firms included in our dataset were as follows: $0.6 billion (2002), $2.6 billion (2003), and $3.2 billion (2004).

Table 7: Bonus Take-Up Rates Across Eligible Investments
tax years, C corporations only

Tax Class	2002	2003	2004
3-year property	56%	58%	62%
5-year property	58%	61%	64%
7-year property	50%	51%	54%
10-year property	44%	49%	55%
15-year property	49%	56%	64%
20-year property	42%	55%	64%
Weighted Average	54%	58%	61%

Table 8: Bonus Take-Up Rates Across Industries
tax year 2004, C corporations only

NAICS Industry	Bonus Deduction	Share	Industry Averages (millions)		
			Eligible Investment	Tax Life	Take-Up Rate
1 agriculture	0.5	0.4%	0.4	7.4	37%
2 finance - insurance	1.7	1.2%	5.2	7.1	40%
3 real estate and rental - except autos	2.4	1.7%	1.3	5.9	41%
4 manufacturing, except transportation equipment	25.8	18.4%	4.5	6.5	49%
5 transportation and warehousing	6.3	4.5%	3.7	6.7	49%
6 construction	1.7	1.2%	0.4	6.0	49%
7 information - except telecommunications	3.9	2.8%	4.9	5.7	51%
8 repair / personal / other services	0.3	0.2%	0.5	6.4	52%
9 professional services (legal, accounting)	1.9	1.3%	0.8	5.6	54%
10 mining	3.2	2.3%	5.5	6.8	59%
11 accomodations and food service	2.3	1.7%	2.7	6.7	63%
12 administrative services and health care	3.8	2.7%	1.1	6.1	63%
13 banks / thrifts / credit intermediaries	12.6	9.0%	6.5	5.9	66%
14 utilities	15.9	11.4%	72.4	16.6	67%
15 information - telecommunications	13.2	9.4%	30.1	7.4	67%
16 retail	4.7	3.4%	6.0	5.9	68%
17 wholesale	16.0	11.4%	2.3	6.4	71%
18 manufacturing - transportation equipment	17.0	12.2%	34.5	5.3	78%
19 real estate and rental - autos only	6.6	4.8%	28.0	4.9	85%
All Firms	**139.9**	**100.0%**	**3.6**	**7.4**	**61%**